AF324209

The Ash

William Heyen

drawings by Kristen Heyen

TAMARACK EDITIONS

"The Ash" first appeared in *Folio: Work in Progress*, edited by John Slathatos and Martin Booth (London, Oxus Press / Sceptre Press, 1977). "The Eternal Ash" first appeared in *Skywriting*. The other four poems appear here for the first time.

Kristen Heyen's drawings were photo-engraved by Ed Plank of Pontiac Engraving, Oswego, N.Y.

Printed in the United States of America by
BANJO PRESS
P.O. Box 455
Potsdam, N.Y. 13676

The Ash

for William McTaggart

THE ASH

"Every minute, every day,
I hate this life.
I hate the trees, I hate the sunsets,
I hate my wife."

A nurse entered the room,
handed my friend his medicine,
a cup of water and two pills,
lithium and thorazine.

Eyes glazed, sedated,
but fists clenched above his sheets:
"I hate the doctors, the meals,
the beds, the stupid illiterates

who work here." I nodded,
but tried to save myself, ignored him,
closed my eyes, thought (for this was May)
of my mountain ash in white bloom,

at home, where I longed to be,
within its perfume-menstrual smell,
pure love mixed with death
mixed with pure swill

mixed with its own being
where, toward our earth's distillate,
airstreams of bees glide maddened
for blossoms of white filth,

thought of hands dipped
into cavities of ambergris,
of tongues licking scented necks,
lips sucking pus, maggots

humming their hymn of blue flame
in a dead animal's lung,
of the rainbow glaze of mucous,
the milky beauty of pond-scum,

of my own oval of flowering ash
in evening air, the powers that sustain
my body's sick-room odors,
the twisted smiles, the sunlit skin

cancers, the hate-vapors drifting
toward my broken friend, who cried
"I hate books, I hate the seasons,
I hate children, I hate the dead."

Where, if ever, will this end?
My friend moves from one ward to another,
embedded, circling lower. For now, outside,
I circle closer to the white ash flower.

THE ASH: ITS END

June, and gone is the flowering mountain ash's
too-full obscene odor,
with which I lived. Only a thin perfume
lingers on the air

after its earthly love where
white blossoms have rusted:
tree at the end of something,
almost pure spirit at its end.

THE ETERNAL ASH

By early August, the mountain ash's each limb
hangs heavy, its berry clusters
already tinged orange and bending its body
almost to breaking. The ash bears,

and will, this light, this weight.
Even at night under the frost stars, each berry
deepens into the ripe flame
autumn means for it to be,

yes, but to know one thing, but know it:
the lord of the whole tree, in time,
unchanged, its changes mine, delusion;
knowing, now, the mystical winter blossom...

And which August is this, anyway? - - this windless
poise of clusters that never fall, but will,
within the living tree that withers, while
ashlight drifts to the earth, petal by petal.

THE FLOWERING MOUNTAIN ASH BERRY

Sperm floating in air,
  the earth to be its bed,
    packed in its wet orange flesh,
      one luminous oval seed.

THE ZENITH ASH

September winds are elsewhere, have missed her.
Now the green oval of the flowering ash flames.
If I do not take her now,
while berry-clusters hemorrhage her limbs. . .

She is the holiness begun with one seed,
Yours, my Lord. Your
summer has burnished her branches
to this brown-black shine. Her

body does not wait. Time
is. If I, in human error, lose her,
even You, my Lord, will curse me:
each seed in each berry a skull's leer.

Now the green oval of the flowering tree
flames. And You are the slanting cancerous rays
of autumn sunlight, and You
the source that takes me, and this my ash of praise.

THE FRIEND

Winter. My friend is not my friend,
probably will not return, raves and drools
oblivious to me, the doctors, the walls,
stares into a labyrinth's dead end

where history and logic die:
"I hate the chairs, the words,
the winds, the bastards
in bed with me all night."

But this time, home again
from visiting him, I stepped
from my car onto the shocked bone
of my body, and walked

into the snow-sheathed tree. No gloves
to touch it, I touched it, caressed it.
Flesh burned into its silhouette,
froze: held fast, I wept in waves

until I heard, at last, my lost friend's song;
Goodby, friend, I will die alone.
Goodby, your body is a wing
as frail as mine.

Alive in its dumb sticks, the tree
flared, ice-white as stars. And You, Lord,
saw, had given me back to myself to see,

to say goodby to my dead friend,
and to love the dead.

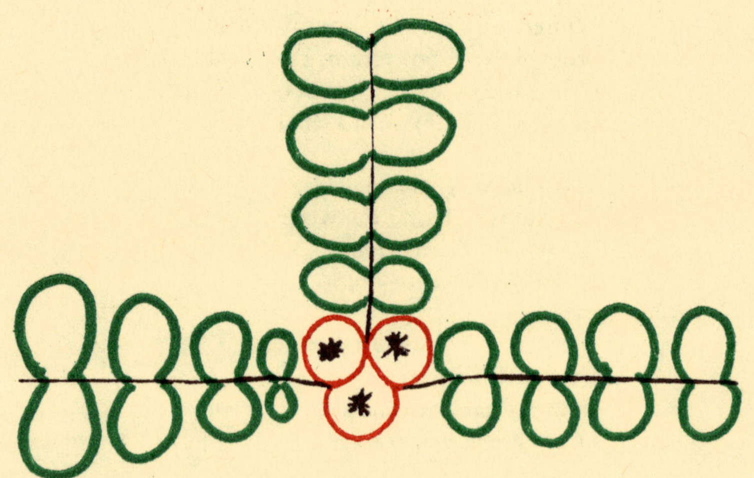

The Ash

Published in an edition of 326 copies, 126 of which contain a
special drawing, hand-colored by Kristen Heyen, signed by the
poet and his twelve year old daughter; numbered 1 to 100 and
lettered A to Z. The remaining copies are numbered 101 to 300.
All lettered copies are reserved for presentation. *The Ash* was
letterpressed in two colors from handset Garamond types on
Curtis Tweedweave stock and sewn into paper wrappers.

This is copy: 258

June 1978